B For Bee

Facts about Bee for Toddlers

Dedicated to

My Husband and Four precious gems Aakash, Adithya, Abishek and Sparsha.
You make me so proud. Always be the best you can be.
-Mommy

B for Bee - Facts about Bees for toddlers

This book is aligned with the national curriculum standards of science. This book introduces Bees, its habitat, its description, its diet and some fun facts for a toddler and for early readers. The images support early readers to understand the text . The repetition of words and phrases help the early readers to Ants specifically using vocabulary.. A perfect gift to give your toddler, made in USA

Picture Credits

Pixabay .com
vecteezy.com

Copyright @ 2020 by Alwina Kindo

Content

____

Name

B For Bee

B

Facts about Bee for Toddlers

Alwina Kindo

Bees are flying insects

Bees have 4 wings, 5 eyes and 6 legs.

Bees live in colonies

Male bees in the hive are called drones

and they do not have a stinger.

Worker bees are females.

Bee's body is divided into **three** parts.

1.Head, 2. Thorax and 3. abdomen

They do all the different tasks needed to

operate and maintain the hive.

An average beehive can hold around

50,000 bees.

Honey bees harvest nectar and pollen from flowering plants.

A bee spends all her life time to produce a teaspoon of honey
which is almost 5 grams.

The flavor of the honey determines on the type of the flower the bee takes the nectar from

A Queen Bee can produce 2,000 eggs a day.

Fertilised eggs become female bees

Unfertilised eggs become
male bees

To get more bees in your garden, grow more flowers.

Bees love blue and love cluster plants like lavender and rosemary.

Bees don't want to sting you because they die.

There are over 20,000 different species of bee, found on every continent except Antarctica.

Honey has been shown to have many health benefits

Honey suppresses cough in children

Honey is extremely moisturizing and hydrates even the driest of skin

The darker the honey the better.

The bee is the only social insect to be partially domesticated by humans.

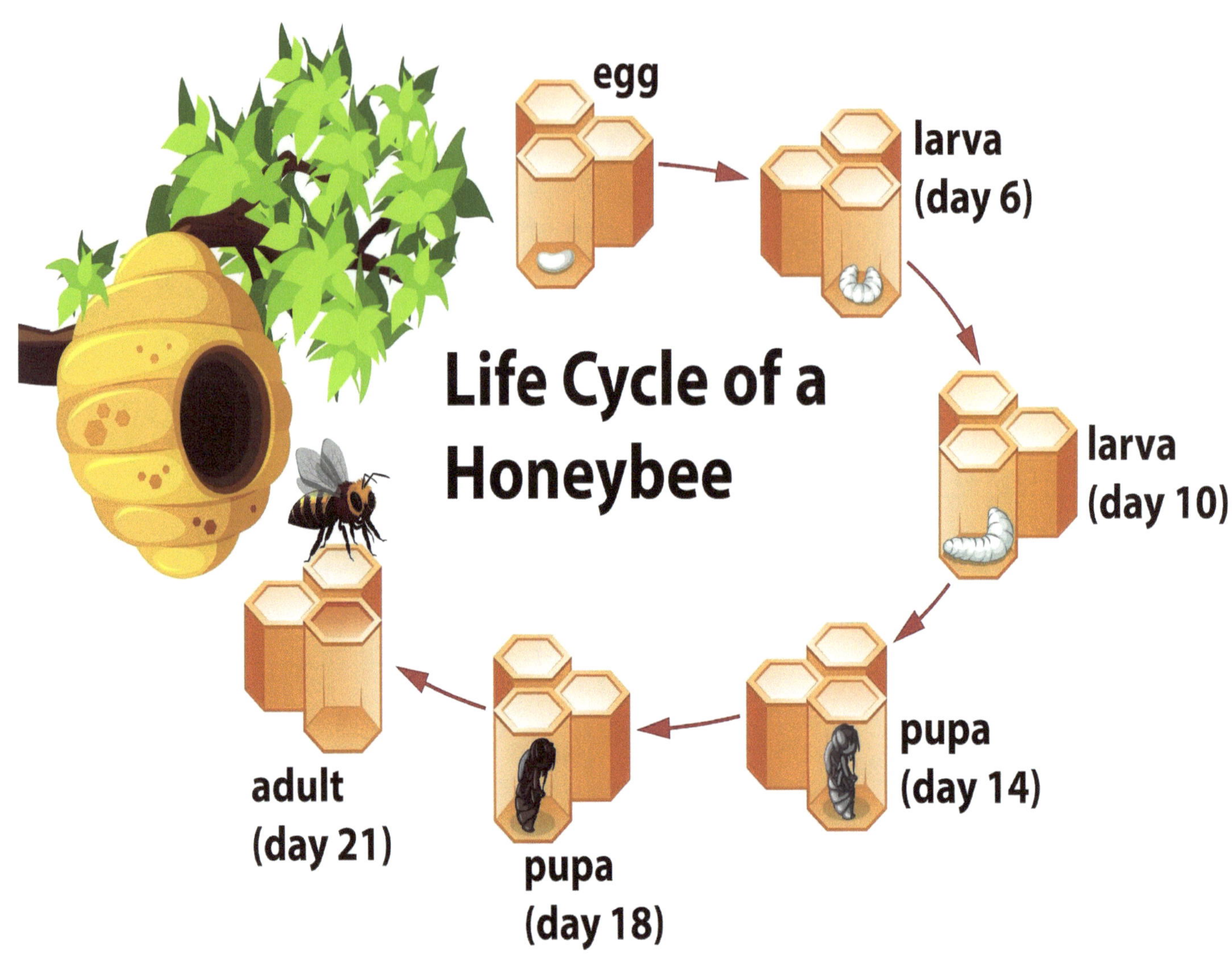

Life cycle of a bee.

Help me find my home!!!

What is this shape?

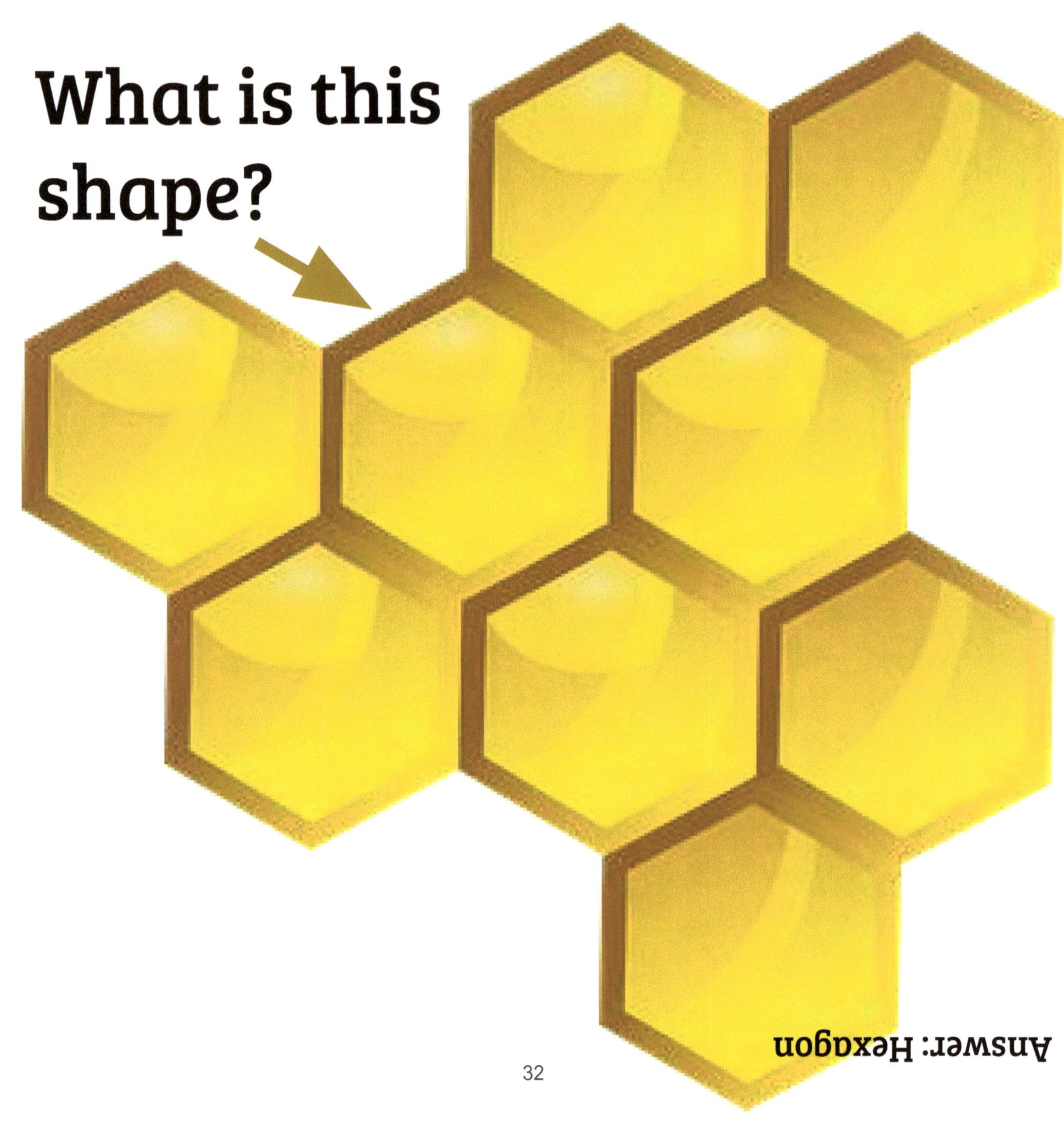

Happy Honey
23 22 21 20 19 18 17 16 15 14 13 12 11 10 9 8 7 6 5 4 3 2 1
Honey
Can you count with me?

This is
to
certify that
____
Name

has read this
book and knows
about bees
____
Completion date

Hope you enjoyed this book.
Check out our other books

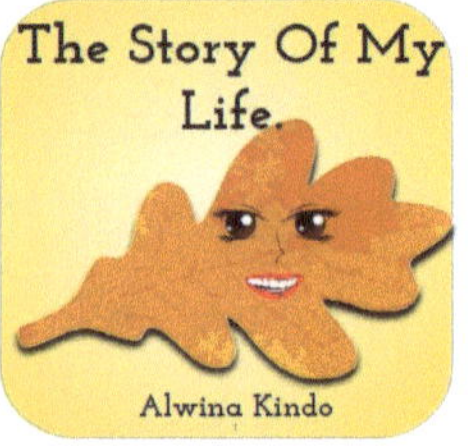

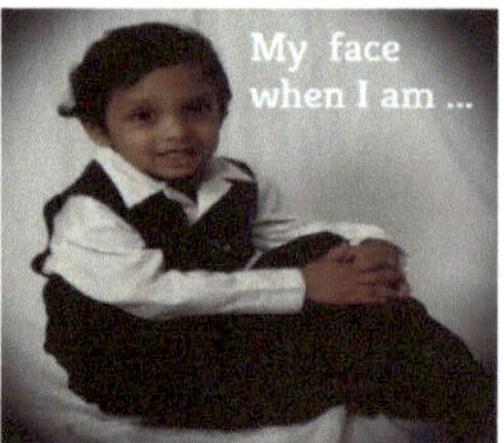

Check out my other books

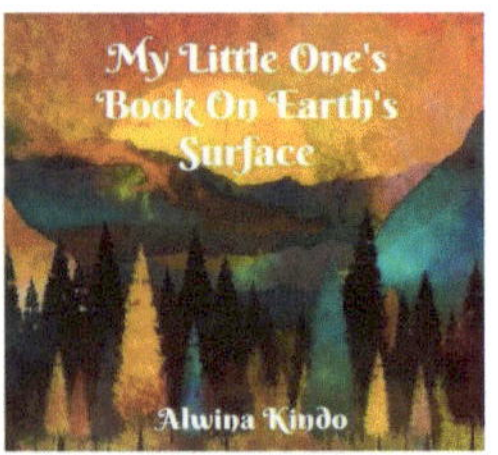

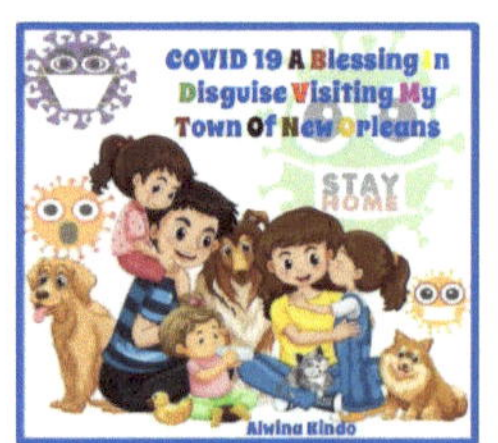

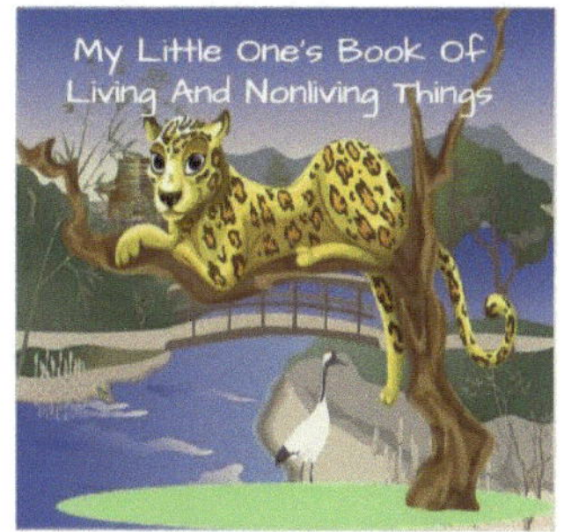

Check Out My Other Books

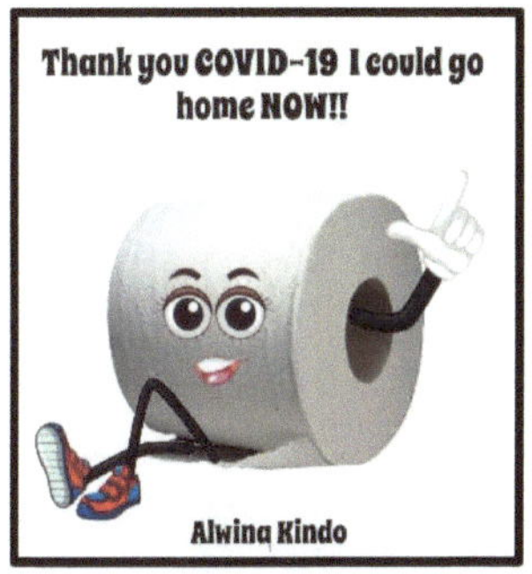

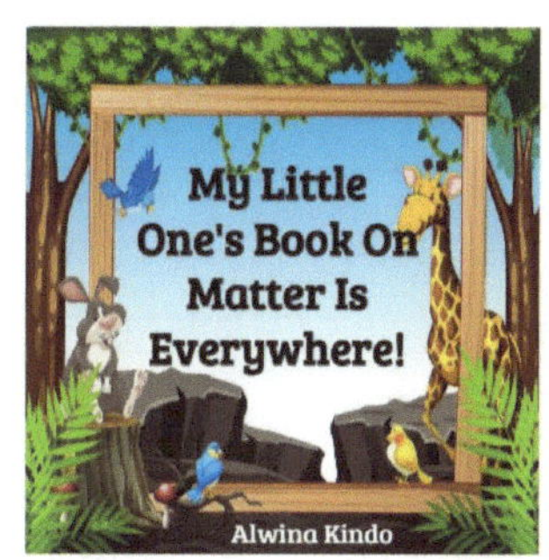

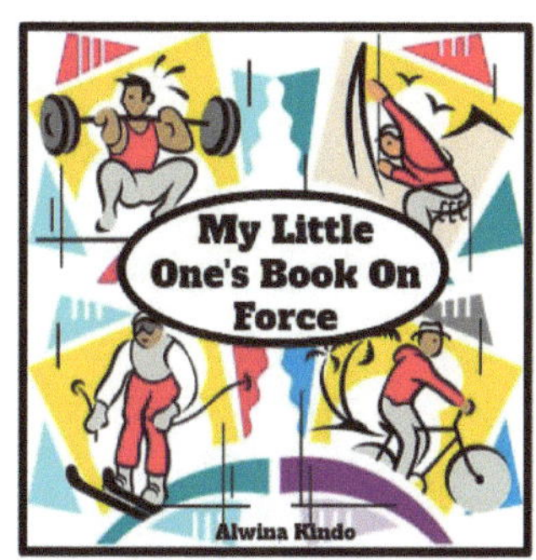

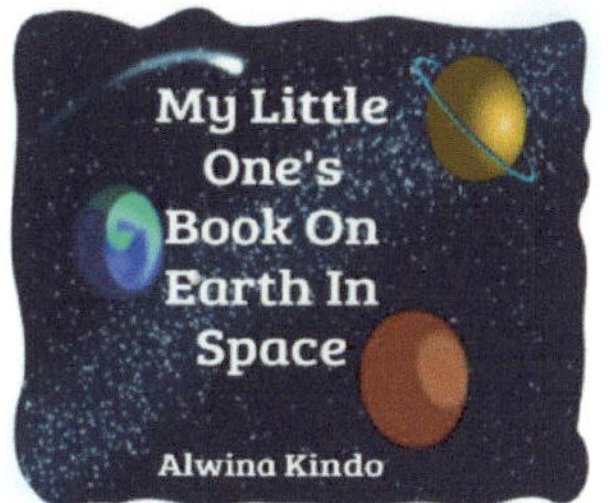